START-UP
ENGLISH
BIOGRAPHIES

◀━━━ • • • • • • • • • • • • • • • • ━━━▶

MARY
SEACOLE

John Malam

Evans Brothers Limited

Published by Evans Brothers Limited
2A Portman Mansions
Chiltern Street
London W1U 6NR

© in this edition Evans Brothers Limited 2009

Printed in China

Editor: Bryony Jones
Designer: Mark Holt

British Library Cataloguing in Publication Data

Malam, John, 1957 –
Mary Seacole. – (Start-up English. Biographies)
1. Seacole, Mary, 1805-1881 – Juvenile literature. 2. Nurses – Jamaica – Biography – Juvenile literature. 3. Crimean War, 1853-1856 – Women – Juvenile literature.
I. Title II. Series
610.7'3'092-dc22

ISBN-13: 9780237538736

Picture acknowledgements: cover (main) Getty Images, (top left and right) Bodleian Library, University of Oxford. (shelfmark 249 t 548), Mary Evans Picture Library; title page Amoret Tanner Collection; **page 1** National Library of Jamaica; **page 5** Travel Ink; **page 6** Mary Evans Picture Library; **page 7** (top) Mary Evans Picture Library (bottom) National Library of Jamaica; **page 8** Bridgeman Art Library/ City of Bristol Museum and Art Gallery, Avon/Private Collection; **page 9** Bridgeman Art Library; **page 10** Robert Harding Art Picture Library; **page 11** Bridgeman Art Library/Private Collection; **page 12** Amoret Tanner Collection; **page 13** Mary Evans Picture Library; **page 14** Bridgeman Art Library/Victoria & Albert Museum, London; **page 15** istock photo; **page 16** (top) Courtesy of the Director, National Army Museum, London (middle) National Library of Jamaica; **page 17** Bridgeman Art Library/Greater London Council; **page 18** Mary Evans Picture Library; **page 19** The Illustrated London News Picture Library; **page 20** Bodleian Library, University of Oxford. (shelfmark 249 t 548); **page 21** (top) Getty Images (bottom) Sascha Rooij

VISIT OUR WEBSITE
Evans
www.evansbooks.co.uk

Contents

Who is Mary Seacole?

Mary Jane Seacole was a nurse and healer. She looked after people in many parts of the world.

During the Crimean War in Europe, she cared for soldiers who were sick and wounded. She became famous for her work. This is her story.

nurse   healer   Crimean War

Mary was born in 1805. Her father was from Scotland. Her mother was a black healer from Africa. Mary had a brother called Edward and a sister called Louisa.

The family lived on an island called Jamaica in the Caribbean Sea.

Mary's family

When Mary's mother was young, she was taken from her home in Africa to Jamaica. She did not want to go. On Jamaica she was a slave, like thousands of other black people. After a while she was given her freedom back. She was lucky.

► Slaves in Jamaica worked in the sugar cane fields.

slave   freedom

Mary's family were quite well off.

▶ Mary and her family lived in Kingston, a port in Jamaica.

◀ Mary's mother owned a big house like this one. People paid money to stay there when they were ill. Mary's mother looked after them.

well off   owned   port   7

Mary visits England

As a child, Mary heard stories about faraway places. She wanted to visit them.

When she was twelve, Mary went to England. She went across the sea in a big boat and landed in Bristol. She visited London and met her father's family for the first time.

faraway

▲ England was not at all like
Jamaica. London was a much bigger city than
Kingston. To Mary it seemed cold, grey and smoky.

Because there were not many black people, Mary
looked different. When she was older, Mary wrote
about how children had made fun of her.

city

Learning about medicine

Mary's mother made medicines from plants. Mary helped her, and learned a lot of useful things. Jamaica is hot and wet. Lots of plants grow there.

We do not know if Mary went to school. We know she played at being a nurse. She pretended that her pets were ill and made them better.

medicines   pretended

After visiting England Mary went back home to Jamaica. She began to make jams and pickles to sell. She used the money to pay for other trips.

▲ Mary visited other islands in the West Indies by boat. She learned about the plants healers used in all the places she went to.

pickles   islands   West Indies

Marriage and work

When Mary was thirty-one she married Edwin Seacole. Now her name was Mrs Seacole. But her new husband died soon after.

Mary worked harder than ever. She made medicines that cured people of horrible diseases like yellow fever and cholera.

cured   diseases   yellow fever

In 1850 Mary visited her brother in Panama. She travelled on horseback, like the people in this picture, who are crossing a river in Panama.

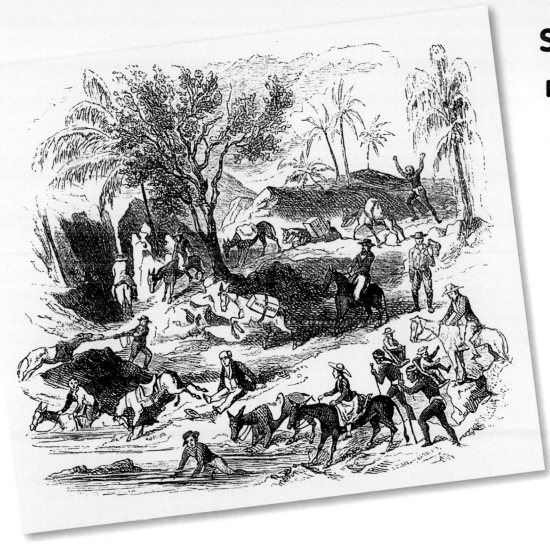

She worked as a nurse and continued to make medicines.

cholera   Panama

War breaks out

Mary heard about a war in Europe. Britain, France and Turkey fought against Russia, in an area called the Crimea. The war was the Crimean War.

▲ This is a painting of the war.

Lots of Mary's soldier friends were sent to fight in the war.

▶ Many were hurt, and Mary wanted to nurse them.

She went to London, hoping she would be sent to work as a nurse. But she was told she could not go. Mary went anyway, paying with her own money. She set sail in January 1855, and arrived in the Crimea in the summer.

soldier

How did Mary help?

Mary set up a **canteen** and **store** for the soldiers. It is on the left of the picture. It was a wooden hut and she called it the British Hotel.

◀ **The hut was also a shop. Mary is the lady in the hat.**

canteen   store

Many soldiers were hurt in the war. There were 'hospitals' in tents, but they were very dirty. Mary helped the soldiers even when there was fighting all around. This was very dangerous.

▼ Nurses worked all through the night. They used lamps like the one in this picture to help them see.

tents   dangerous   17

'Mother Seacole'

Mary gave the soldiers food, medicine and love. People in Britain read in the newspapers about her hard work. "She is always on the battlefields," one writer said.

► The soldiers were always pleased to see Mary. She called them 'her sons' and they called her 'Mother Seacole'.

battlefields

After the war, Mary went to London. She was given **medals** to thank her for looking after the soldiers.

▶ This picture shows the end of the war. Mary is in the middle of the line of people, wearing a fine hat with a feather.

Mary had no money left but she had many friends. They organised a huge music show to help her **raise** money.

Mary the famous nurse

Mary wrote a book about her life. It was called 'Wonderful Adventures of Mrs Seacole'

In her book Mary said she came back from the war "wounded, as many people did". This meant she felt hurt by the soldiers' suffering. But she was glad she had gone. Mary spent the rest of her life in Jamaica and England.

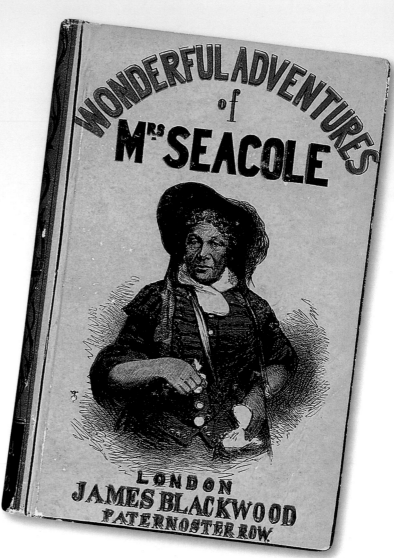

suffering

She was so famous as a nurse that Queen Victoria asked her to help her son when he was ill.

▼ Mary died in 1881. She was buried in London.

▲ In 2005 the only known portrait of Mary Seacole was discovered.

Today Mary is remembered as one of the world's most famous nurses.

buried

Further information for

Key words introduced in the text

battlefields	dangerous	Jamaica	pretended	West Indies
buried	diseases	medals	raise	wounded
canteen	Europe	medicines	slave	yellow fever
cared	faraway	nurse	soldier	
cholera	fought	owned	store	
city	freedom	Panama	suffering	
Crimean War	healer	pickles	tents	
cured	islands	port	well off	

Background Information

Mary Seacole

Mary Seacole (1805-1881) was a nurse and healer who is known for her work during the Crimean War. Mary learnt many of her skills, in particular how to make medicines from plants, from her mother who was a black healer from Africa. She also travelled extensively in Central America and Europe, where she developed her knowledge of medicine further. When Mary heard about the war in Europe she went to London offering her services. She was not included however in the group of 38 women nurses, led by Florence Nightingale, who went to the Crimea in 1854. It is likely that racial prejudice played a key role in this decision. Determined to go anyway, Mary funded the trip using her own money and set up the British Hotel where she cared and provided for injured soldiers. When the war ended, Mary returned to England, bankrupt. She had many friends and supporters in Britain who held fundraising events in her honour. She remained a famous nurse for the rest of her life and died in 1881.

The Crimean War

The Crimean War (1854-6) was fought between Russia and the Allied forces of Turkey, Britain and France. The war has become known for incompetent leadership as shown, for example, in the Charge of the Light Brigade. Within weeks of British troops arriving in Turkey, thousands of them were struck down with cholera and malaria. Many more soldiers died of disease than of their war wounds, due to the disgusting conditions in the army hospitals: while 4,600 British soldiers were killed in battle, over 17,500 died of disease. The war was eventually won by the Allies, although at considerable cost in terms of lives lost and political and military careers ruined.

Remembering Mary

During her lifetime Mary received high praise and recognition for her work as a healer. But after her death she was forgotten for nearly a century, her work overshadowed by that of Florence Nightingale. Nurses from the West Indies and Africa came together in 1981 to make her name known again. In 2003 a campaign was launched for a permanent memorial to Mary

Parents and Teachers

Seacole in London – she was left out of the original Crimean War Memorial. In 2004 Mary came first in a poll of 100 Great Black Britons. A year later, the only known portrait of Mary was discovered. It is on display in the National Portrait Gallery, in London.

Topics for discussion

Imagine running a store for the soldiers like Mary did. What would the soldiers want to buy?

What do you think the differences are between being a nurse during Mary's time and being a nurse today?

Mary played at being a nurse as a child. What job might you want to do when you are older?

Suggested activities

Find out about other famous women from the 19th century. Compare Mary Seacole's life with that of Florence Nightingale. Make a wall map showing all the places that Mary travelled to. Write a short biography of a family member or friend.

Recommended resources

Hoorah for Mary Seacole (Hopscotch Histories) Trish Cooke and Anni Axworthy, Fanklin Watts 2008
Start-Up History: Florence Nightingale Stewart Ross, Evans, 2002
The Wonderful Adventures of Mrs Seacole in Many Lands Mary Seacole, Penguin Classics, 2005

http://www.maryseacole.com

Important dates

1805	Mary Jane Grant was born in Kingston, Jamaica
1817	Age 12 – she visited London for the first time
1836	Age 31 – she married Edwin Horatio Seacole
1843	Age 38 – her house in Kingston burnt down
1850	Age 45 – she went to Panama, in Central America
1854	The Crimean War started in Europe
1855	Age 50 – she went by ship to the Crimea
1856	The Crimean War ended. Mary went back to London
1857	Age 52 –she wrote her book. It was called 'Wonderful Adventures of Mrs Seacole'
1881	Age 76 – she died and was buried in London
2005	The only known colour portrait of Mary Seacole was discovered. It is on display in the National Portrait Gallery in London

Index